AF615184

The Wisdom of George Herbert

Compiled by

Nick Page

LION
Giftlines

Published by
Lion Publishing plc
Sandy Lane West, Oxford, England
www.lion-publishing.co.uk
ISBN 0 7459 4077 3

First edition 1999
10 9 8 7 6 5 4 3 2 1 0

A catalogue record for this book is available from the British Library

Typeset in 10/12 Baskerville
Printed and bound in Singapore

Designer: Philippa Jenkins
Artwork: Amanda Barlow

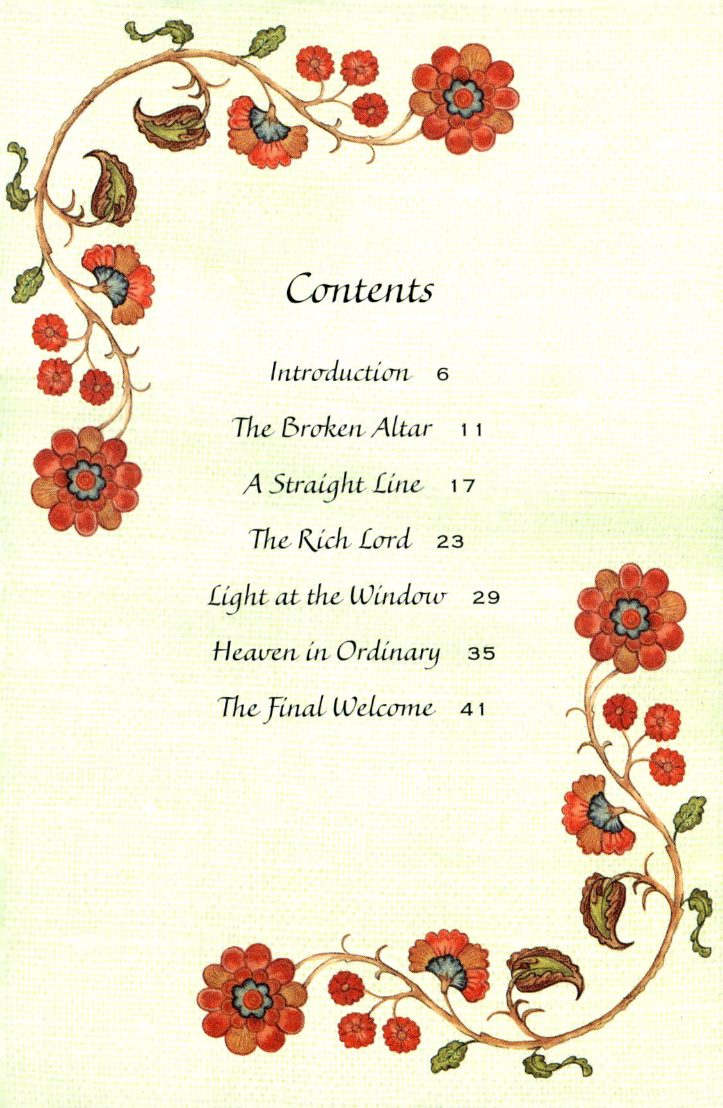

Contents

Introduction

George Herbert died young. He published few poems in his lifetime, and those were in Latin. Ambitious in youth, he spent his final years in the obscurity of a small country parish. Yet Herbert left the world a legacy of writing that continues to influence and inspire people today, and, some 400 years after his death, Herbert is acknowledged as one of the greatest devotional poets of all time.

Writers as diverse as Vaughan, Cowper, Coleridge, Gerard Manley Hopkins, T.S. Eliot and C.S. Lewis have admitted his influence. John Wesley was responsible for reprinting some of his poems. Herbert's small volume of advice to parish priests (originally published as *The Priest to the Temple* but universally known by the simpler, more fitting title of *The Country Parson*) still has much to say to us about the Christian life.

Herbert was born in 1593 into an aristocratic family in Montgomery, Wales. His mother, the intelligent and beautiful Magdalene Herbert, was a friend of John Donne and the subject of Donne's poem 'The Autumnal'. His elder brother Edward, as well as writing volumes of philosophy and poetry, became Ambassador to France. His father died when George was three, and the family lived the next few years on the move, eventually settling

in London. A gifted scholar, Herbert attended first Westminster School and then Trinity College, Cambridge.

From an early age he appears to have been torn between a career at court and the life of a cleric. He felt God's call to the ministry, but was nevertheless attracted to the secular world. After taking his degree he became Public Orator to the University in 1619, a job which required him to make speeches and write letters on behalf of the University of Cambridge to all manner of royalty and dignitaries.

In 1626 he was ordained. There is no indication that this was a decision to embrace the church; it was merely in fulfilment of University regulations which stated that all Fellows were expected to take holy orders. Similarly, although he was officially Rector of Leighton Bromswold, this post was little more than a sinecure. He began the rebuilding of the church but he appears to have been an infrequent visitor to the parish. His hopes were still for secular influence, but the doors were closed. After eight years, he resigned as Orator. Despite contact with the court and people of influence, his hopes of preferment came to nothing. After a brief spell as a Member of Parliament, he drifted aimlessly, uncertain of which direction to turn.

'Were it not better to bestow/Some place or power on me?' he asks in his poem 'Submission'. But in his heart he knew the truth: that he could only find true happiness in the place where he believed God meant him to be. Eventually, dogged by ill-health, he answered the call which he had been hearing for years.

In 1630 he became a parish priest; rector of the wonderfully named rural parish of Fuggleton-cum-Bemerton, near Salisbury. This was no honorary post but a real vocation. The church was badly in need of repair (John Aubrey described it as a 'pitifull little chapel of Ease') and even today visitors are surprised by how small the chapel is, with room for scarcely more than thirty people.

It was unusual for a man of Herbert's rank and family background to become a priest at all, let alone rector of such a humble church. He had always been viewed as somewhat haughty and proud of his descent; but perhaps that was ultimately his reason for going to Bemerton. He had tried the glory of the world; now he served the glory of God. He had no illusions. He knew that his profession was viewed with what he called 'general ignominy', but he believed that to serve in such a place was to know more of Christ, since 'he must be despised; because this hath been the portion of God his master and of God's saints his brethren, and this is foretold, that it shall be so still, until things be no more'.

The last three years of his life were spent in serving his parishioners. During this time he wrote his treatise *The Country Parson*, which sets forth the duties and responsibilities of the parish priest. He married. He worked on his poetry, reshaping and reordering it. And he was content. Perhaps he finally understood the pattern. After years of struggle, he had come home. There was only one more journey to take: he died in 1633 at the age of thirty-nine.

At first sight, it was a quiet life. No wars, no battles, no weighty affairs of state. But this very quietness points to the enduring qualities of Herbert's work. For his struggles were against himself; the battles he fought were between what he wanted to do and what he thought he wanted to do. It is a conflict that many of us undergo. We know what we want to do, we know what we should do, but which should we choose? Herbert's spiritual journey speaks to us today because it is true to our own experience. He was never a poet of pious platitudes, but of the profound struggles of the Christian life.

The simple power of his writing and his mastery of language make his work a joy for all lovers of poetry. His poems reflect simultaneously a profound, abiding faith and a meticulous craftsmanship, some even taking the form of pictures on the page.

Herbert's poems were published after his death as *The Temple*. The book was an immediate success, running through four editions in three years, and was followed in 1652 by *Herbert's Remains*, a book which not only included *The Country Parson* but also the *Outlandish Proverbs*, previously published in 1640, which Herbert had collected and translated throughout his life. In 1670 Izaak Walton published his famous *Life of Mr George Herbert*, a vivid, moving and wildly embellished biography of the poet.

A quiet life, little over 150 poems, some translations, some Latin verse, a handful of letters, a collection of proverbs and a book about being a parson: this does not seem the stuff of literary greatness. But Herbert's was a life of secret glory. He had come through his personal

battles, reconciled himself with what he understood to be God's will for his life, and found happiness in apparent obscurity. 'Who would have thought my shrivelled heart/Could have recovered greenness?' he wrote in his poem 'The Flower'.

> And now in age I bud again,
> After so many deaths I live and write;
> I once more smell the dew and rain,
> And relish versing.

George Herbert's verses are indeed to be treasured and relished. For his struggles are ours, his journey is one we all must take, and his final homecoming is an inspiration to us all.

The Broken Altar

Who spits against heaven,
it falls in his face.

FROM *OUTLANDISH PROVERBS*

The Altar

A broken altar, Lord, thy servant rears,
Made of a heart and cemented with tears;
Whose parts are as thy hand did frame;
No workman's tool hath touched the same.
A heart alone
Is such a stone
As nothing but
Thy power doth cut.
Wherefore each part
Of my hard heart
Meets in this frame
To praise thy name.
That if I chance to hold my peace,
These stones to praise thee may not cease.
Oh, let thy blessed sacrifice be mine,
And sanctify this altar to be thine.

New Creations

Lord, mend or rather make us: one creation
  Will not suffice our turn:
Except thou make us daily, we shall spurn
  Our own salvation.

From 'Giddiness'

Peace

Where there is peace, God is.

FROM *OUTLANDISH PROVERBS*

Easter Wings

Lord, who createdst man in wealth and store,
Though foolishly he lost the same,
Decaying more and more,
Till he became
Most poor:
With thee
O let me rise
As larks, harmoniously,
And sing this day thy victories:
Then shall the fall further the flight in me.

My tender age in sorrow did begin;
And still with sicknesses and shame
Thou didst so punish sin,
That I became
Most thin.
With thee
Let me combine,
And feel this day thy victory;
For, if I imp* my wing on thine,
Affliction shall advance the flight in me.

* *to graft feathers onto an injured wing, thus restoring flight*

Trinity Sunday

Lord, who hast formed me out of mud,
And hast redeemed me through thy blood,
And sanctified me to do good;

Purge all my sins done heretofore:
For I confess my heavy score,
And I will strive to sin no more.

Enrich my heart, mouth, hands in me,
With faith, with hope, with charity;
That I may run, rise, rest with thee.

A Straight Line

Everyone is a
master and servant.

FROM *OUTLANDISH PROVERBS*

The Power of Love

Love is swift of foot;
Love's a man of war,
   And can shoot,
And can hit from far.

FROM 'DISCIPLINE'

Sin

Lord, with what care hast thou begirt us round!
  Parents first season us: then schoolmasters
  Deliver us to laws; they send us bound
To rules of reason, holy messengers,
Pulpits and Sundays, sorrow dogging sin,
  Afflictions sorted, anguish of all sizes,
  Fine nets and stratagems to catch us in,
Bibles laid open, millions of surprises,
Blessings beforehand, ties of gratefulness,
  The sound of glory ringing in our ears:
  Without, our shame; within, our consciences;
Angels and grace, eternal hopes and fears.
  Yet all these fences and their whole array
  One cunning bosom-sin blows quite away.

A Wreath

A wreathed garland of deserved praise,
Of praise deserved, unto thee I give,
I give to thee, who knowest all my ways,
My crooked winding ways, wherein I live,
Wherein I die, not live: for life is straight,
Straight as a line, and ever tends to thee,
To thee, who art more far above deceit
Than deceit seems above simplicity.
Give me simplicity, that I may live,
So live and like, that I may know thy ways,
Know them and practise them: then shall I give
For this poor wreath, give thee a crown of praise.

9

True Riches

He loseth nothing, that loseth not God.
Knowledge is folly, except grace guide it.

FROM *OUTLANDISH PROVERBS*

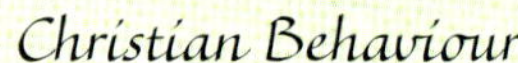

Christian Behaviour

Do all things like a man, not sneakingly:
Think that the king sees thee still; for his King does.

FROM 'THE CHURCH PORCH'

Do well, and right, and let the world sink.

FROM *THE COUNTRY PARSON*

The Rich Lord

All worship is prerogative,
and a flower
Of his rich crown.

FROM 'TO ALL ANGELS AND SAINTS'

Jesu

Jesu is in my heart, his sacred name
Is deeply carved there: but th' other week
A great affliction broke the little frame
Even all to pieces: which I went to seek:
And first I found the corner, where was *J*,
After, where *ES*, and next where *U* was graved.
When I had got these parcels,* instantly
I sat me down to spell them, and perceived
That to my broken heart he was *I ease you*,
And to my whole is *JESU*.

* *fragments, pieces*

Redemption

Having been tenant long to a rich lord,
  Not thriving, I resolved to be bold,
  And make a suit unto him, to afford
A new small-rented lease, and cancel th' old.
In heaven at his manor I him sought:
  They told me there, that he was lately gone
  About some land, which he had dearly bought
Long since on earth, to take possession.
I straight returned, and knowing his great birth,
  Sought him accordingly in great resorts;
  In cities, theatres, gardens, parks, and courts:
At length I heard a ragged noise and mirth
  Of thieves and murderers: there I him espied,
  Who straight, *Your suit is granted*, said, and died.

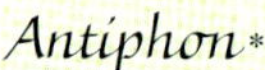

Antiphon*

Chorus Let all the world in every corner sing,
My God and King.

Verse The heavens are not too high,
His praise may thither fly:
The earth is not too low,
His praises there may grow.

Chorus Let all the world in every corner sing,
My God and King.

Verse The church with psalms must shout,
No door can keep them out:
But above all, the heart
Must bear the longest part.

Chorus Let all the world in every corner sing,
My God and King.

* *a hymn sung responsively by two choirs*

The Son

Let foreign nations of their language boast,
  What fine variety each tongue affords:
  I like our language, as our men and coast;
Who cannot dress it well, want wit, not words.
How neatly do we give one only name
  To parents' issue and the sun's bright star!
  A son is light and fruit; a fruitful flame
Chasing the father's dimness, carried far
From the first man in th' East, to fresh and new
  Western discoveries of posterity.
  So in one word our Lord's humility
We turn upon him in a sense most true;
  For what Christ once in humbleness began,
  We him in glory call *The Son of Man*.

Love-joy

As on a window late I cast mine eye,
I saw a vine drop grapes with *J* and *C*
Annealed* on every bunch. One standing by
Asked what it meant. I (who am never loth
To spend my judgment) said, It seemed to me
To be the body and the letters both
Of *Joy* and *Charity*. Sir, you have not missed,
The man replied; it figures *JESUS CHRIST*.

* *process of fixing colours by heating glass*

Light at the Window

A man that looks on glass,
On it may stay his eye;
Or if he pleaseth, through it pass,
And then the heaven espy.

FROM 'THE ELIXIR'

The Windows

Lord, how can man preach thy eternal word?
He is a brittle crazy* glass:
Yet in thy temple thou dost him afford
This glorious and transcendent place,
To be a window, through thy grace.

But when thou dost anneal in glass thy story,
Making thy life to shine within
The holy preacher's; then the light and glory
More reverend grows, and more doth win:
Which else shows waterish, bleak, and thin.

Doctrine and life, colours and light, in one
When they combine and mingle, bring
A strong regard and awe: but speech alone
Doth vanish like a flaring thing,
And in the ear, not conscience ring.

* *cracked, flawed*

17

Thankfulness

Thou that hast given so much to me,
Give one thing more, a grateful heart.

FROM 'GRATEFULNESS'

Church Music

Sweetest of sweets, I thank you: when displeasure
  Did through my body wound my mind,
You took me thence, and in your house of pleasure
  A dainty lodging me assigned.

Now I in you without a body move,
  Rising and falling with your wings:
We both together sweetly live and love,
  Yet say sometimes, *God help poor Kings.*

Comfort, I'll die: for if you post from me,
  Sure I shall do so, and much more:
But if I travel in your company,
  You know the way to heaven's door.

Friendship and Love

Now love is his business and aim; wherefore he likes well, that his parish at good times invite one another to their houses, and he urgeth them to it: and sometimes, where he knows there hath been or is a little difference, he takes one of the parties, and goes with him to the other, and all dine or sup together. There is much preaching in this friendliness.

FROM *THE COUNTRY PARSON*

Sunday

O day most calm, most bright,
The fruit of this, the next world's bud,
Th' endorsement of supreme delight,
Writ by a friend, and with his blood;
The couch of time; care's balm and bay:
The week were dark, but for thy light:
Thy torch doth show the way.

FROM 'SUNDAY'

Heaven in Ordinary

The country parson is exceeding
exact in his life, being holy, just,
prudent, temperate, bold,
grave in all his ways.

FROM *THE COUNTRY PARSON*

Christian Work

Neither praise nor dispraise thyself; thy actions serve the turn.

FROM *OUTLANDISH PROVERBS*

Who is the honest man?
He that doth still and strongly good pursue,
To God, his neighbour and himself most true:
Whom neither force nor fawning can
Unpin, or wrench from giving all their due.

FROM 'CONSTANCY'

Who sweeps a room as for thy laws,
Makes that and th' action fine.

FROM 'THE ELIXIR'

Prayer

Prayer the Church's banquet, angels' age,
  God's breath in man returning to his birth,
  The soul in paraphrase, heart in pilgrimage,
The Christian plummet sounding heaven and earth;
Engine against th' Almighty, sinner's tower,
  Reversed thunder, Christ-side-piercing spear,
  The six-days' world transposing in an hour,
A kind of tune, which all things hear and fear;
Softness, and peace, and joy, and love, and bliss,
  Exalted manna, gladness of the best,
  Heaven in ordinary, man well dressed,
The milky way, the bird of Paradise,
  Church-bells beyond the stars heard, the soul's blood,
  The land of spices; something understood.

In Church

When once thy foot enters the church, be bare.
God is more there, than thou: for thou art there
Only by his permission. Then beware,
And make thyself all reverence and fear.

FROM 'THE CHURCH PORCH'

Resort to sermons, but to prayers most:
Praying's the end of preaching.

FROM 'THE CHURCH PORCH'

Sermons are dangerous things.

FROM *THE COUNTRY PARSON*

Simple Truth

The parson's yea is yea, and nay, nay; and his apparel plain, but reverend and clean, without spots, or dust, or smell; the purity of his mind breaking out, and dilating itself even to his body, clothes and habitation.

FROM *THE COUNTRY PARSON*

Blessed Be the Poor

But perhaps being above the common people, our credit and estimation calls on us to live in a more splendid fashion? – but O God! how easily is that answered, when we consider that the blessings in the holy Scripture are never given to the rich, but to the poor. I never find Blessed be the Rich, or Blessed be the Noble; but *Blessed be the Meek*, and *Blessed be the Poor*, and *Blessed be the Mourners, for they shall be comforted*.

FROM A LETTER QUOTED IN WALTON'S *LIVES*

The Final Welcome

God is at the end,
when we think
he is furthest off it.

FROM *OUTLANDISH PROVERBS*

26

Seeing God in All

Teach me, my God and King,
In all things thee to see,
And what I do in anything
To do it as for thee.

From 'The Elixir'

Virtue

Sweet day, so cool, so calm, so bright,
The bridal of the earth and sky;
The dew shall weep thy fall tonight,
    For thou must die.

Sweet rose, whose hue angry and brave
Bids the rash gazer wipe his eye;
Thy root is ever in its grave,
    And thou must die.

Sweet spring, full of sweet days and roses,
A box where sweets compacted lie;
My music shows ye have your closes,
    And all must die.

Only a sweet and virtuous soul,
Like seasoned timber, never gives;
But though the whole world turn to coal,
    Then chiefly lives.

At Night

Sum up at night what thou hast done by day;
And in the morning, what thou hast to do.
Dress and undress thy soul: mark the decay
And growth of it: if with thy watch, that too
  Be down, then wind up both; since we shall be
  Most surely judged, make thy accounts agree.

FROM 'THE CHURCH PORCH'

Praise day at night, and life at the end.

FROM *OUTLANDISH PROVERBS*

The Way, Truth and Life

Come, my Way, my Truth, my Life:
Such a Way, as gives us breath:
Such a Truth, as ends all strife:
And such a Life, as killeth death.

FROM 'THE CALL'

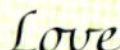

Love

Love bade me welcome: yet my soul drew back,
Guilty of dust and sin.
But quick-eyed Love, observing me grow slack
From my first entrance in,
Drew nearer to me, sweetly questioning,
If I lacked anything.

A guest, I answered, worthy to be here.
Love said, You shall be he.
I, the unkind, ungrateful? Ah my dear,
I cannot look on thee.
Love took my hand, and smiling did reply,
Who made the eyes but I?

Truth, Lord, but I have marred them; let my shame
Go where it doth deserve.
And know you not, says Love, who bore the blame?
My dear, then I will serve.
You must sit down, says Love, and taste my meat.
So I did sit and eat.

Select Bibliography

The Temple, 1633
Outlandish Proverbs, 1640
Remains (including most of *A Priest to the Temple*, and *Jacula Prudendum* – a revised version of *Outlandish Proverbs*), 1652
A Priest to the Temple, or The Country Parson, His Character and Rule of Holy Life, 1671

Acknowledgments

cover, 1: St Mary Magdalene by Guido Reni; © National Gallery, London
2: Portrait of George Herbert by Hamish Moyle
11: The Purification of the Temple, after Michelangelo; © National Gallery, London
13: BEN110325 The Virgin Sewing, from the Cappella dell'Annunciata (Chapel of the Annunciation) 1610 (photo) by Guido Reni (1575–1642); Palazzo del Quirinale, Rome/Bridgeman Art Library, London/New York
14: An Angel, attributed to Giovanni Battista Moroni; © National Gallery, London
17: Christ Washing his Disciples' Feet by Jacopo Tintoretto; © National Gallery, London
21: FIT86013 Madonna and Child, c. 1628 (panel) by Sir Anthony van Dyck (1599–1641); Fitzwilliam Museum, University of Cambridge/ Bridgeman Art Library, London/New York
23: Three Female Musicians by an unknown 16th-century artist: SuperStock Ltd
29: St John the Baptist in the Wilderness, attributed to Bartolomé Esteban Murillo; © National Gallery, London
31: St Jerome by Guido Reni; © National Gallery, London
35: A Donor by a follower of Quinten Massys; © National Gallery, London
41: MAM68667 Lament of Christ by the Virgin and St John, 1614/15 (panel) by Peter Paul Rubens (1577–1640); Kunsthistorisches Museum, Vienna/Bridgeman Art Library, London/New York
42: A River Landscape by Joris van der Haagen; © National Gallery, London
45: Christ as the Light of the World by Paris Bordone; © National Gallery, London
47: Christ Embracing St John the Baptist by Guido Reni; © National Gallery, London